THINGS I'VE THOUGHT

(I THINK)

STEVEN TWIGG

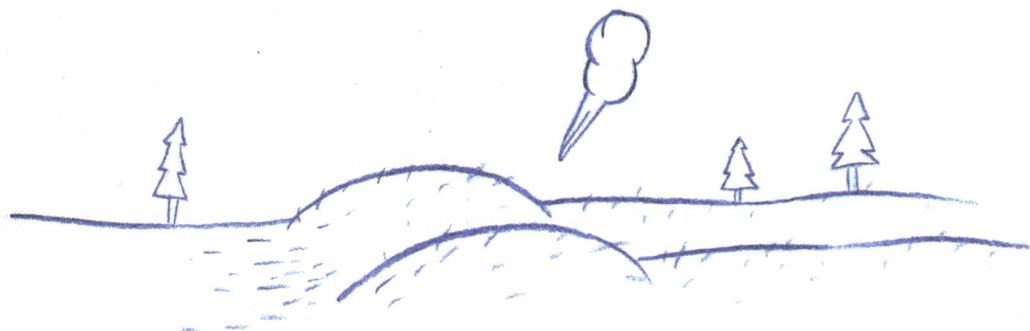

DEDICATED TO DEDICATION.
I COULDN'T HAVE DONE THIS WITHOUT YOU.

WHY GEEKS LOVE ARGYLE...

FULL MOON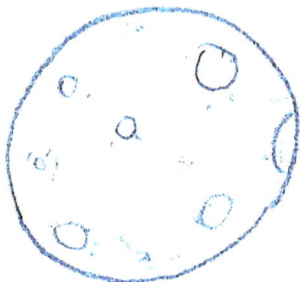

HALF MOON

QUARTER MOON

8AM-BREAKFAST

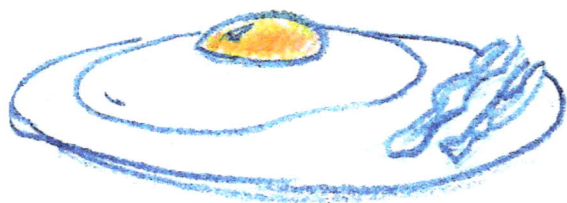

6PM-DINNER

QUESTION ANSWERED.

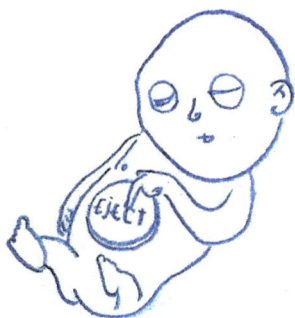

VENN DIAGRAM OF THINGS I ENJOY

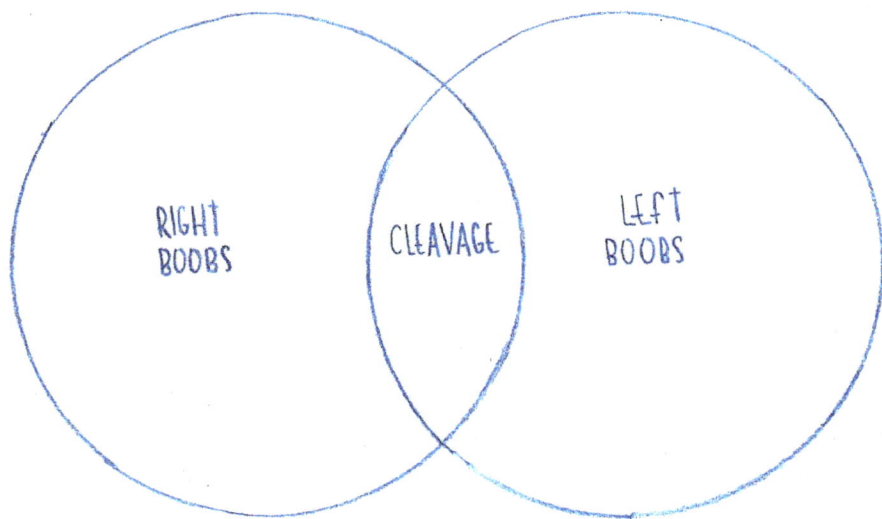

RIGHT
BOOBS

CLEAVAGE

LEFT
BOOBS

I TRIED MAKING ICE-CREAM ONCE
BUT IT TOOK TOO LONG
AND I'M LACTOSE-IMPATIENT

I BUILT A TIME-MACHINE,
BUT IT WAS A WHILE FROM NOW...

I ALWAYS EAT WITH MY HANDS,
IN FACT THEY GO EVERYWHERE WITH ME.

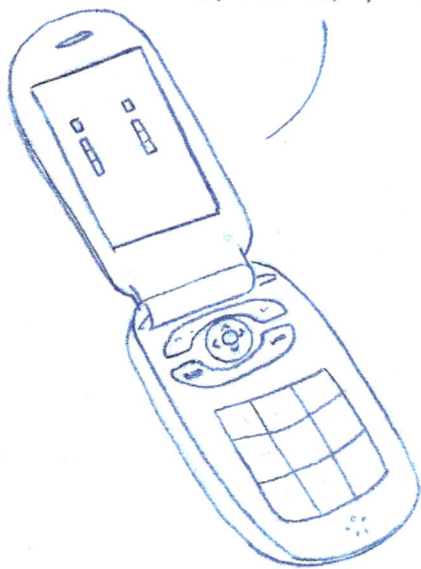

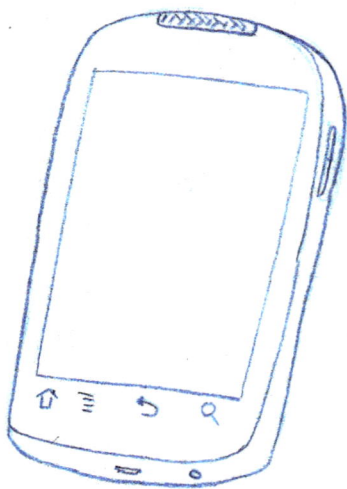

twenty-dollar
Bill

PHONIX ST

COFFIN

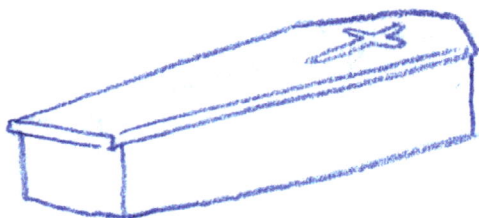

COFFOUT

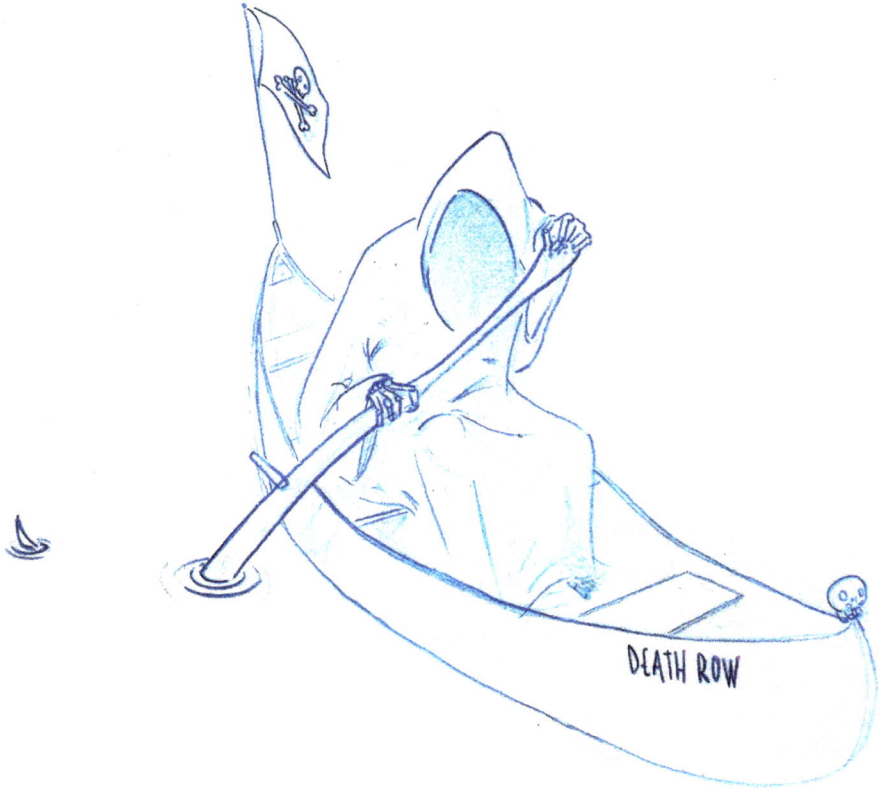

ONE DAY I TOOK A BUS DOWNTOWN...
NEVER EVEN GAVE IT BACK.

I DON'T REMEMBER ANY FRENCH NOW
BUT AT ONE TIME I NOUS SOMMES.

NEVER BOOK A JUDGE BY THEIR COVER.

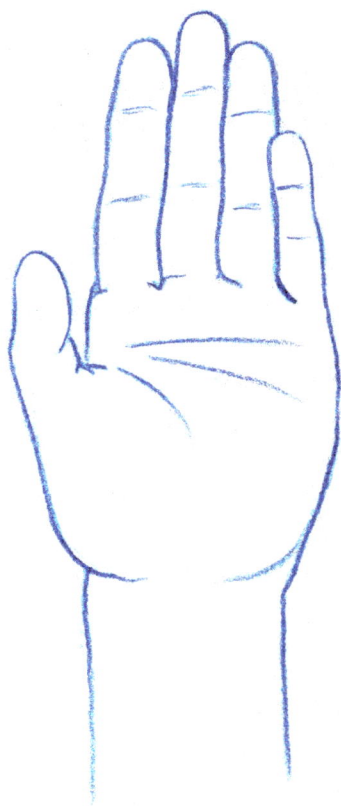

ROCK-ON   ROCK-OFF

EAST 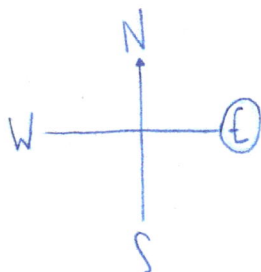 EASTER  EASTEST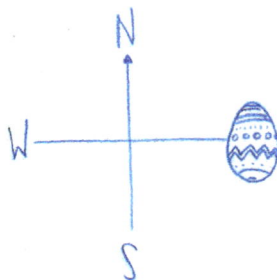

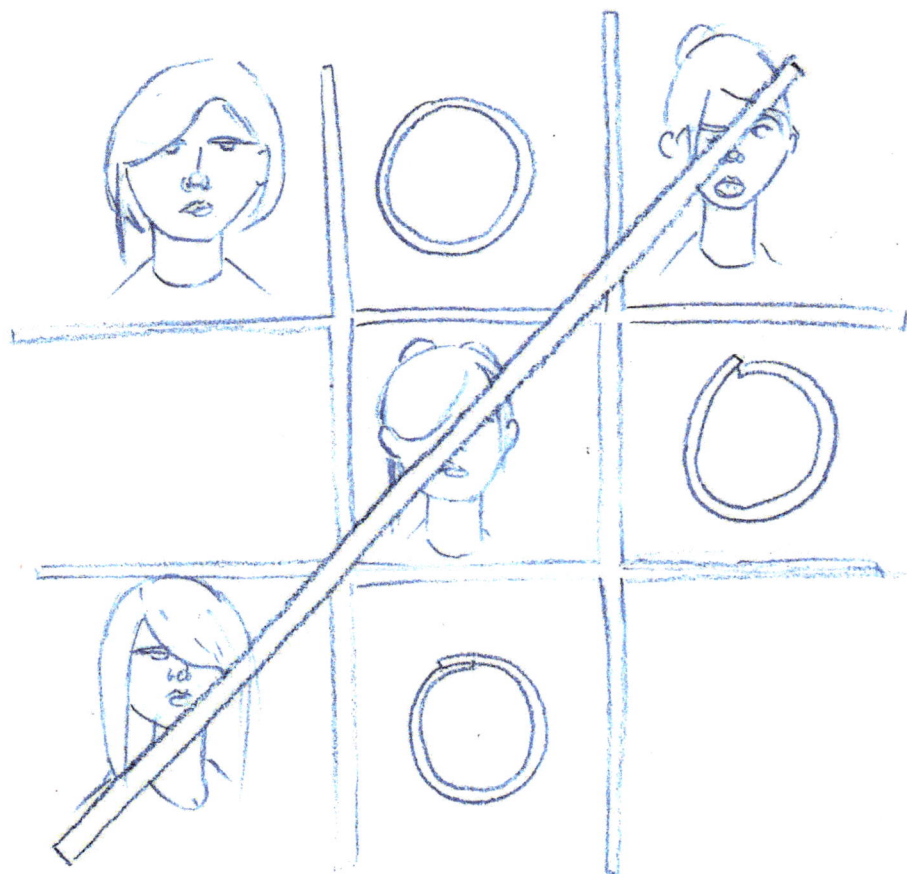

GAME OF EX'S AND O'S

GARDEN HOE

GAS CAN

GAS CAN'T

CANNON BALLS

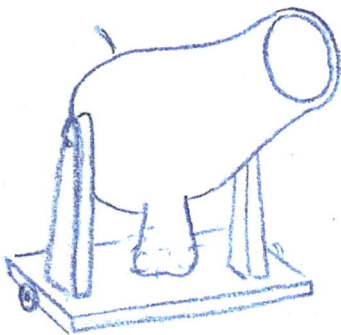

PADDLE BALLS

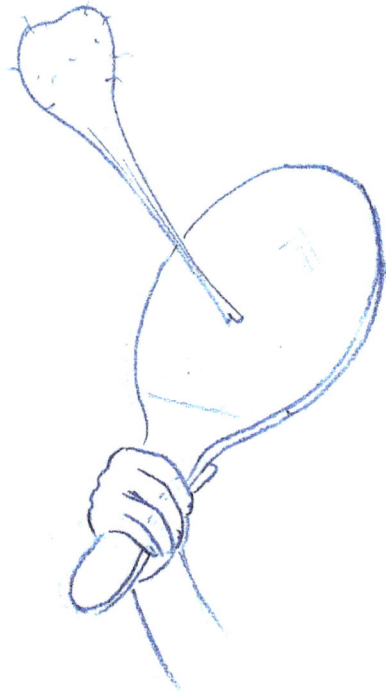

BASKET BALLS

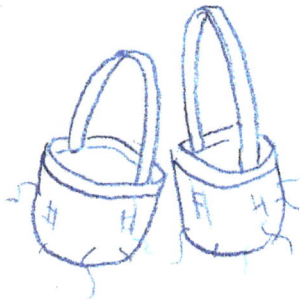

I WENT OUT SHOPPING FOR CHRISTMAS
BUT EVERYWHERE WAS SOLD-OUT,
SO I BOUGHT A HANUKKAH.

LOANS ARE AN INTERESTING THING.

I WAS GOING TO GET AN 80'S HAIRCUT
BUT THEN I THOUGHT I'D MULLET OVER.

NINJA

NUNJA

DISCOURAGING GARBAGE CAN
OUTSIDE JUGGLING SCHOOL

GOLDFISH

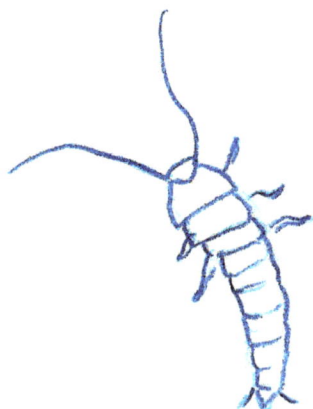

SILVERFISH

BRONZEFISH

SELFISH

THINGS TO BE THANKFUL FOR:
- UNICORNS
- MY FAMILY
- THAT THIS PEN STILL WORKS
- SCREW THIS

I HATE P.D.I. (PUBLIC DISPLAYS OF INFECTION)

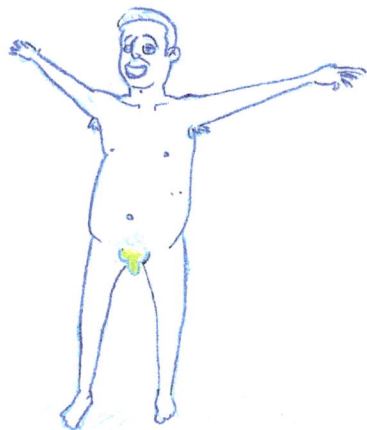

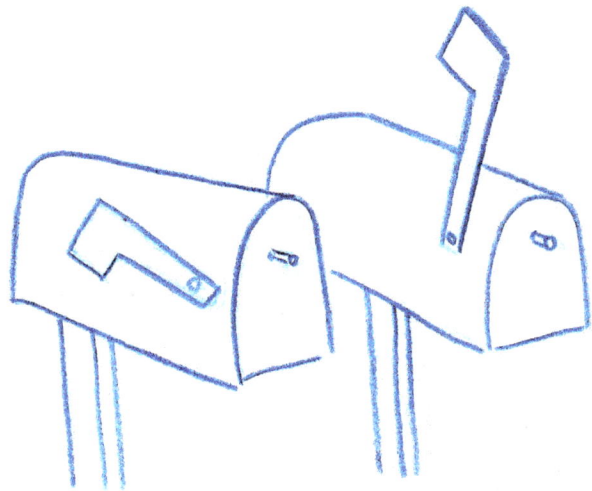

NO MAIL.   MAIL.

NO WIND.   WIND.

ROBOT SUICIDES

THINGS A PICK-UP TRUCK WAS
MADE TO HELP YOU PICK-UP:

ROCKS ✓
FURNITURE ✓
GIRLS ✗

MEDIOCRE SOAKER!™

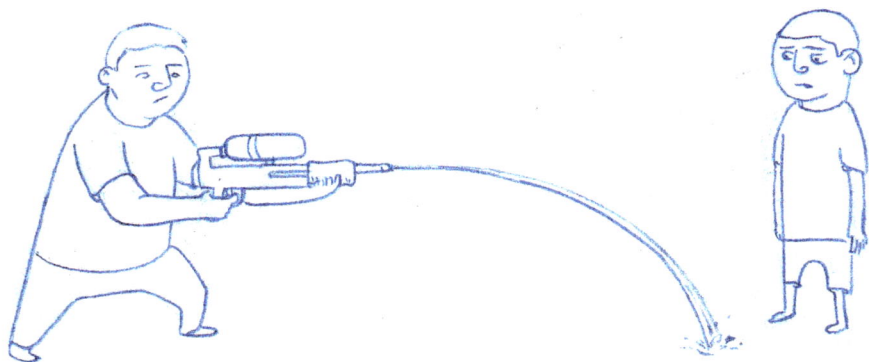

FEDORA THE
EXPLORER

tattoot

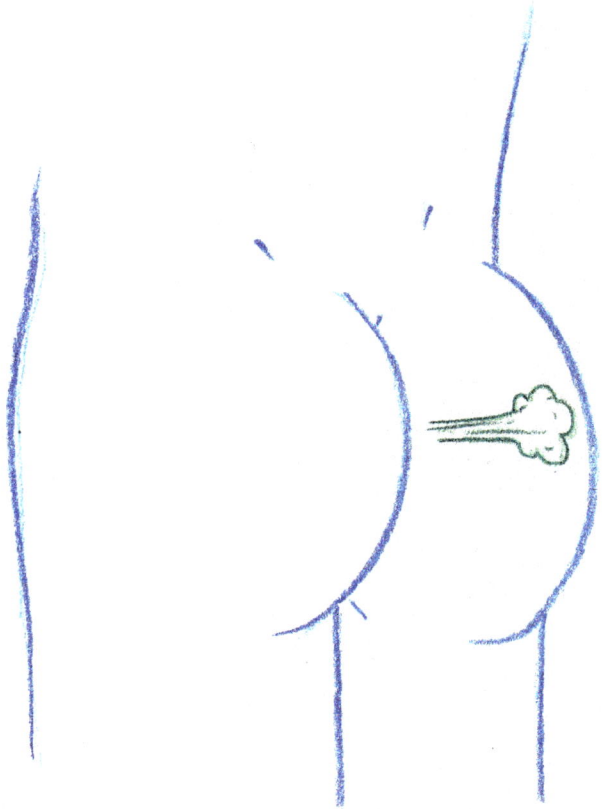

VOLCANOES ARE EARTH'S PIMPLES.

I CAN ASSEMBLE WINDOWS AND
CUPBOARDS BUT DOORS ARE SOMETHING
I COULD NEVER GET A HANDLE ON.

I TRY WITH ALL MY HEART
TO PUMP BLOOD.

"OOPSY DAISY!"
(ALWAYS USE PROTECTION)

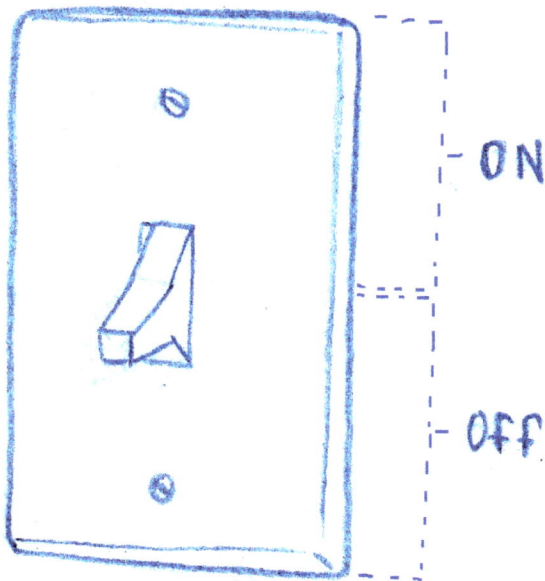

HUMAN BEING

HUMAN BEEN

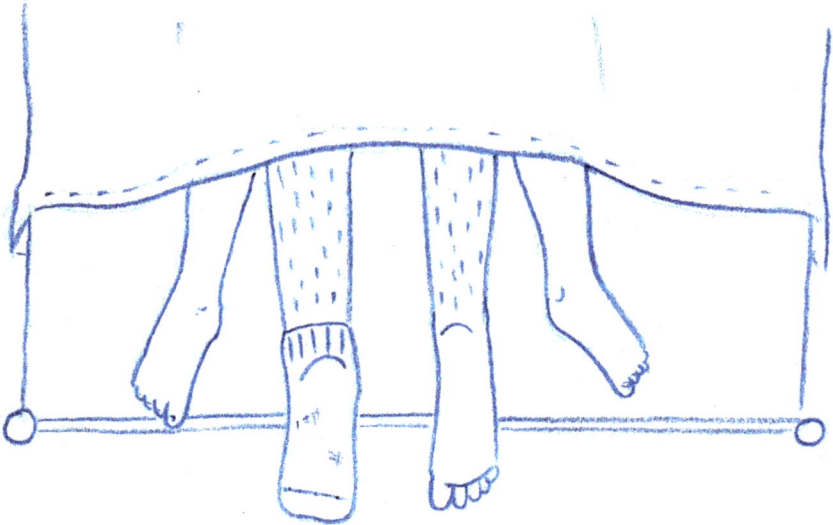

SOCKWARD

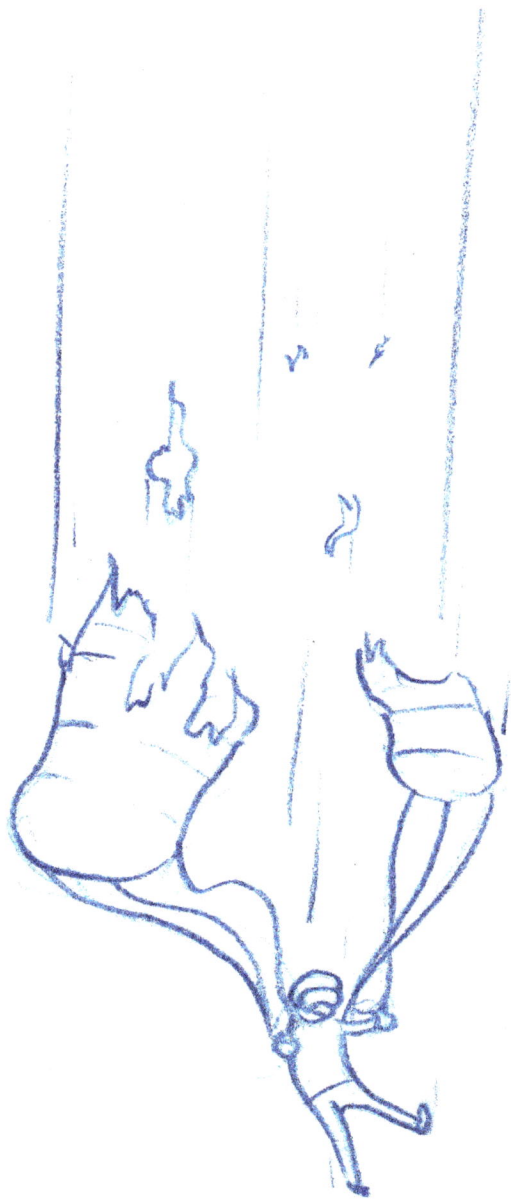

"PARASHIT"

EASLE

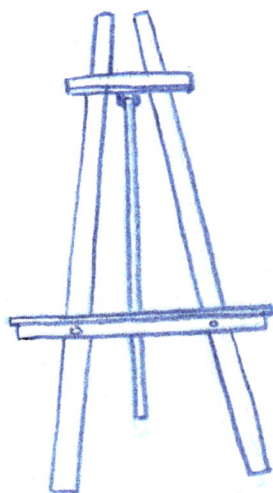

DIFFICULTLE (PICASSO'S)

ONE MAN'S JUNK IS ANOTHER MAN'S HOMOSEXUAL DESIRE.

I DON'T THINK GHOSTS SHOULD BE ALLOWED IN THE LIVING ROOM.

BEWARE OF AVANT-GARDE DOG.

MT. RUSH EVEN MORE

TO BE COMPLETED: YESTERDAY.

URBAN TUMBLEWEED

BUFFA-LOW RIDER

INFAMOUS CUBAN-CIGARGOYLE

MUMMIES... SCARY.   ZOMBIES...SCARY.
GHOSTIES? ...KIND OF CUTE.

I THINK MOUNT EVEREST'S POPULARITY
IS AT ITS PEAK.

I THINK MY RELATIONSHIP WITH
SCOTCH IS ON THE ROCKS.

AIR FRESHENERS IN THE FUTURE

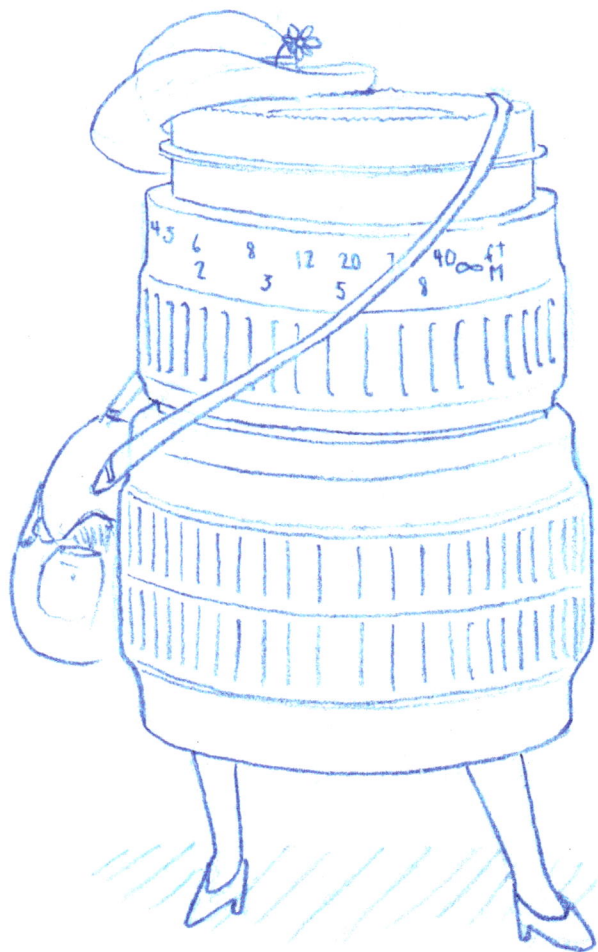

LENS-FLAIR

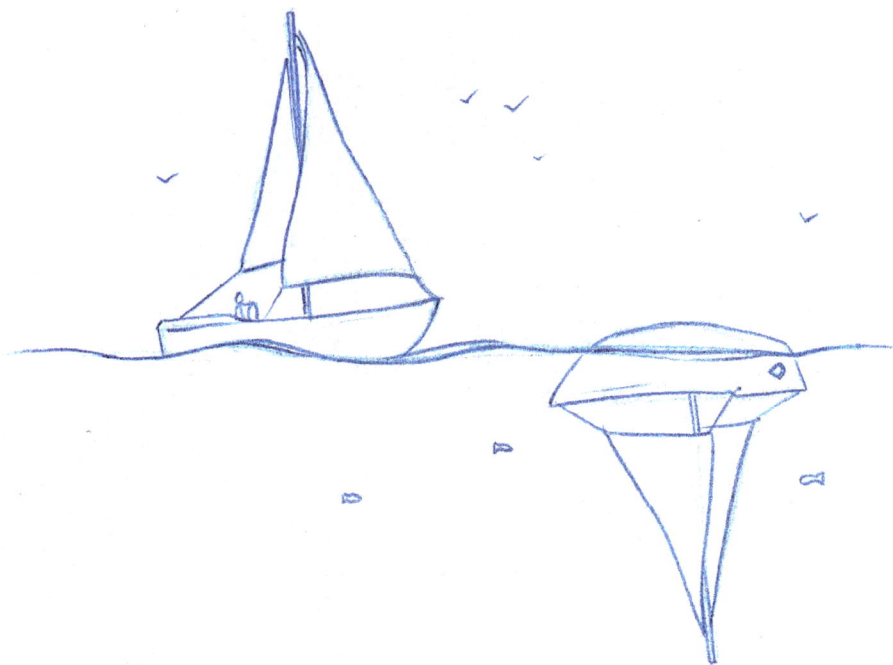

SAILBOAT

fAILBOAT

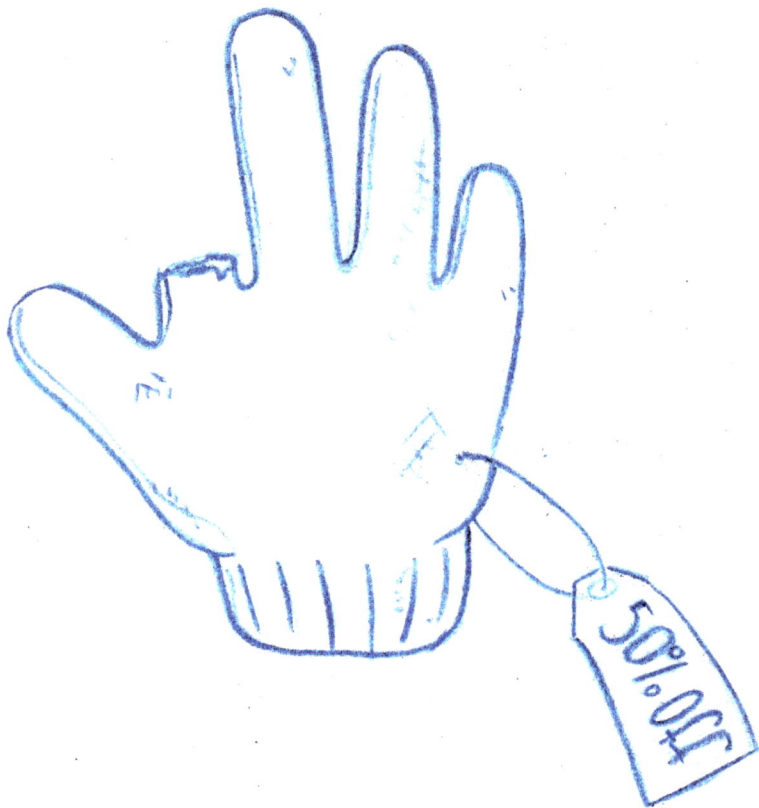

FOUR-FINGER DISCOUNT

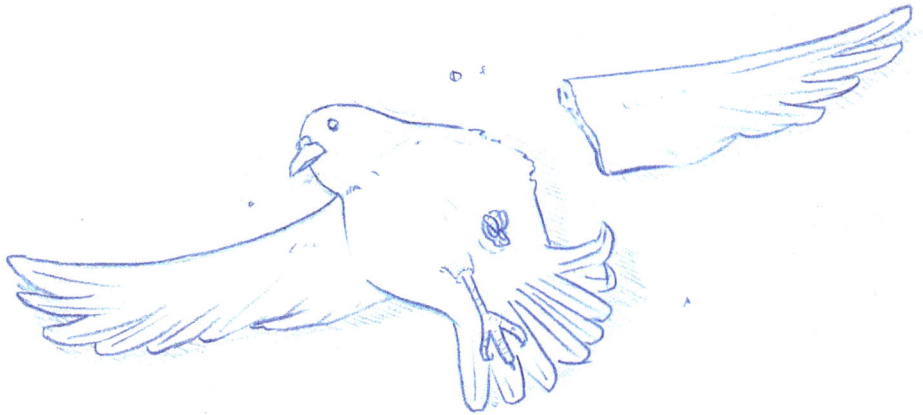

PIECE DOVE

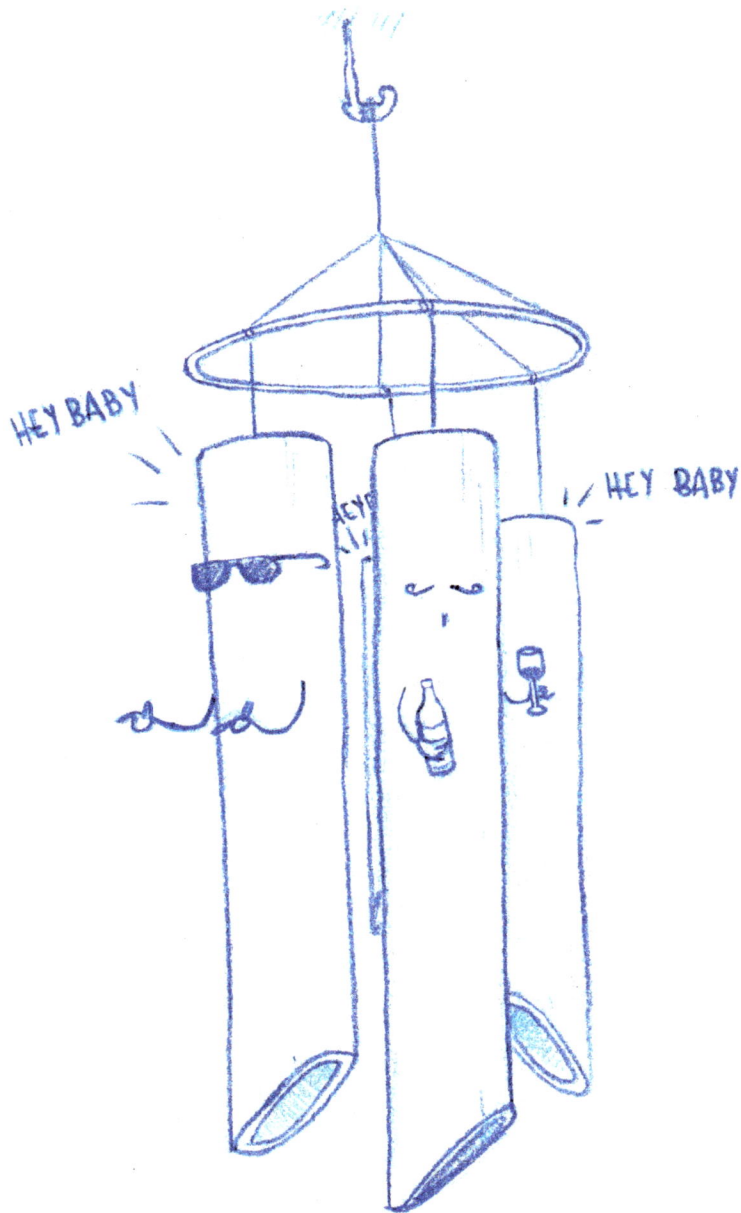

HEY BABY

HEY BABY

WIND CHARMS

GHOSTS HAVE THE WORST POKER-FACES.
YOU CAN SEE RIGHT THROUGH THEM!

DON'T KNOCK A DOOR-KNOCKER
'TIL YOU'VE TRIED IT.

"I'M TRYING, CUT ME SOME SLACK!"
- TIGHTROPE-WALKER'S LAST WORDS.

ALADDIN'S LAUNDRY

KING THONG!

(LARGELY UNDOCUMENTED)

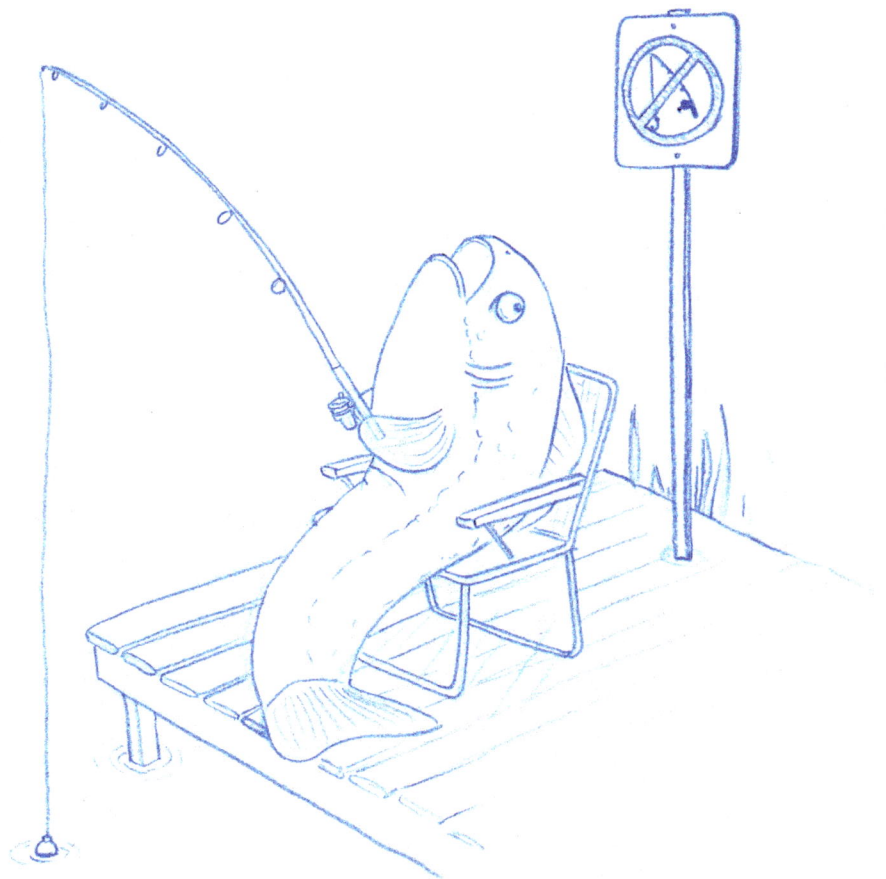

TODAY I CAUGHT A BASS FISHING.

(THAT AWKWARD PHASE)

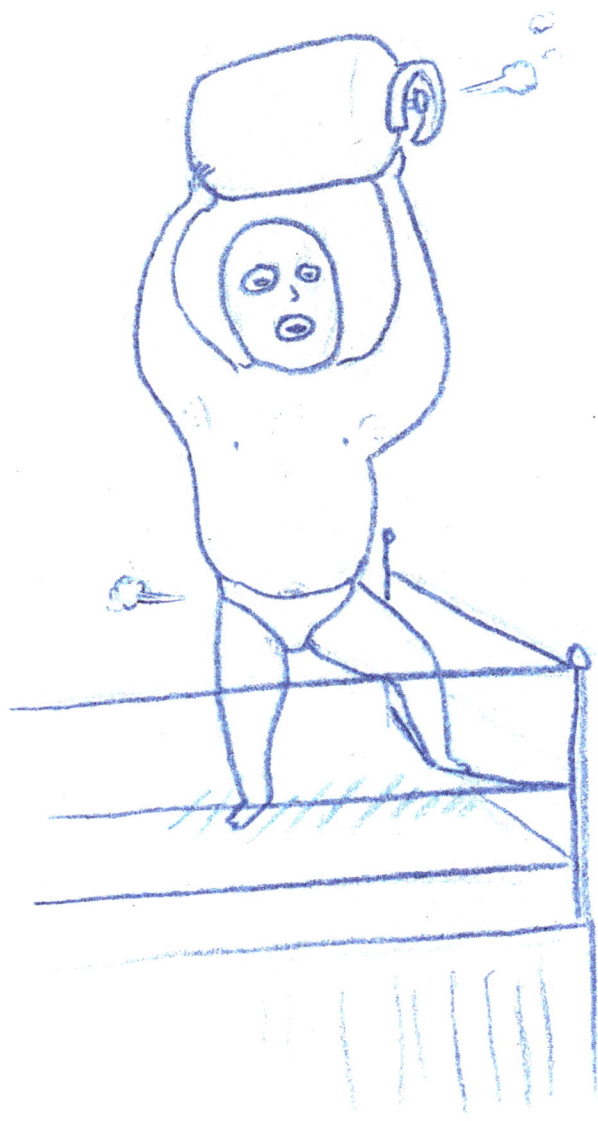

PRO-PAYNE

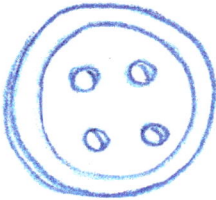

BUTTON   BUTT-ON

CURTAINS (DRAWN)

CURTAINS (NOT DRAWN)

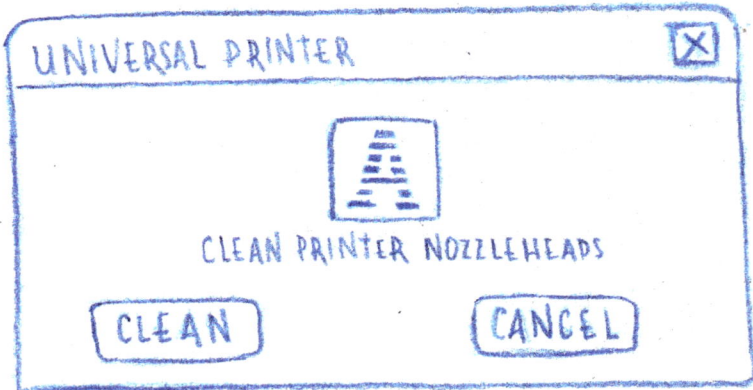

UNIVERSAL PRINTER ☒

CLEAN PRINTER NOZZLEHEADS

CLEAN   CANCEL

I HEARD THERE'S NO SUCH
THING AS RUMORS.

SPHERES ARE POINTLESS.

I HAD FORGOTTEN WHAT
BOOMERANGS DO
THEN IT CAME BACK TO ME.

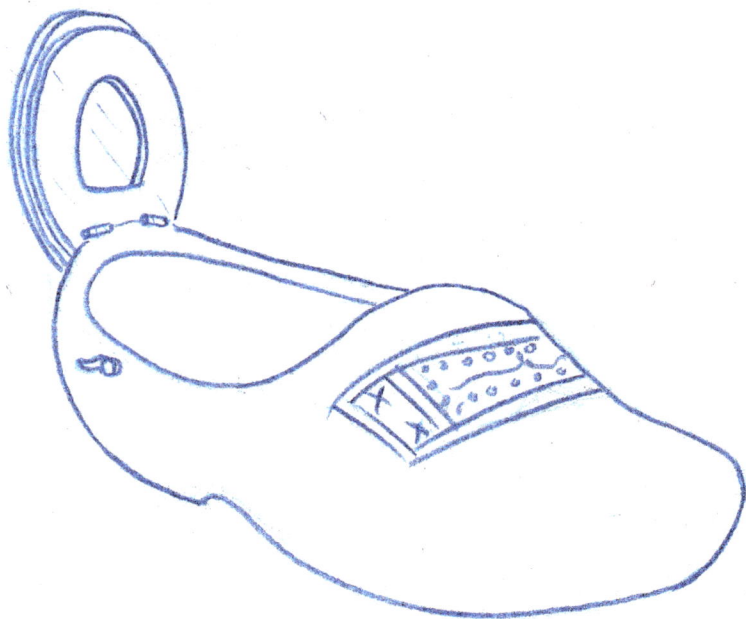

TOILET CLOG

HEY, WHO PUT THAT NOOSE THERE?
I KNOW IT DIDN'T JUST HANG ITSELF!

WAXING IS A RIP-OFF.

EVENTUALLY PETER PAN DID DIE AND
AFTER MANY YEARS BECAME DUST PAN.

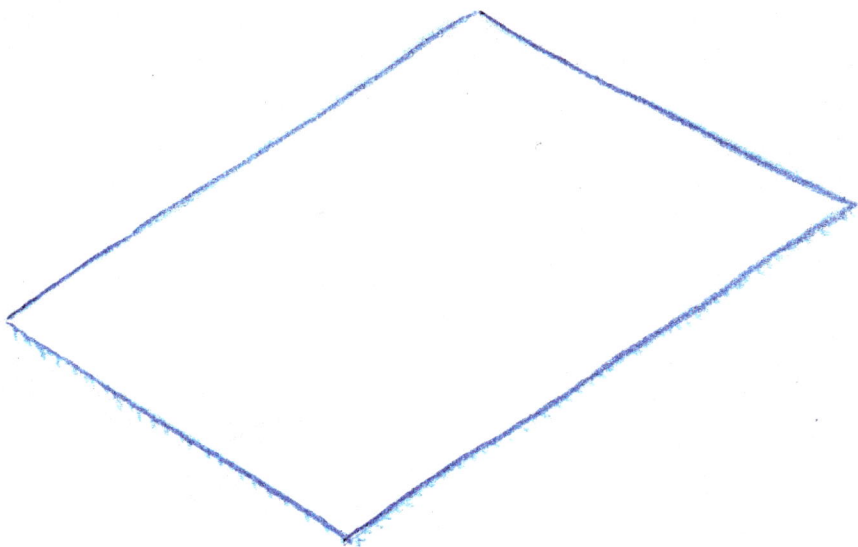

ORIGAMI CRACKER

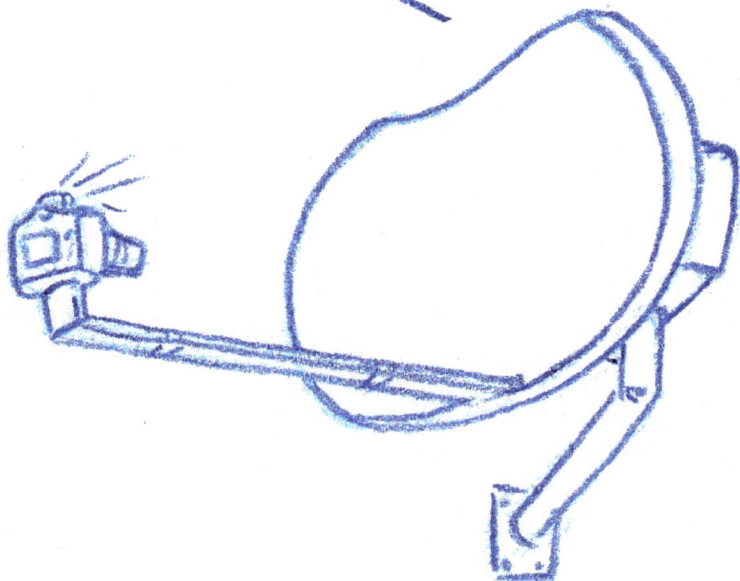

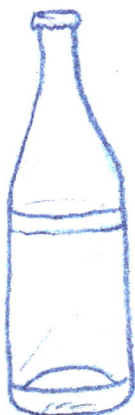

TONE - ALE

RAINBOW STOUT

TREE LAGER

WALT DIZZY
(HUNDRED ACHING WOODS)

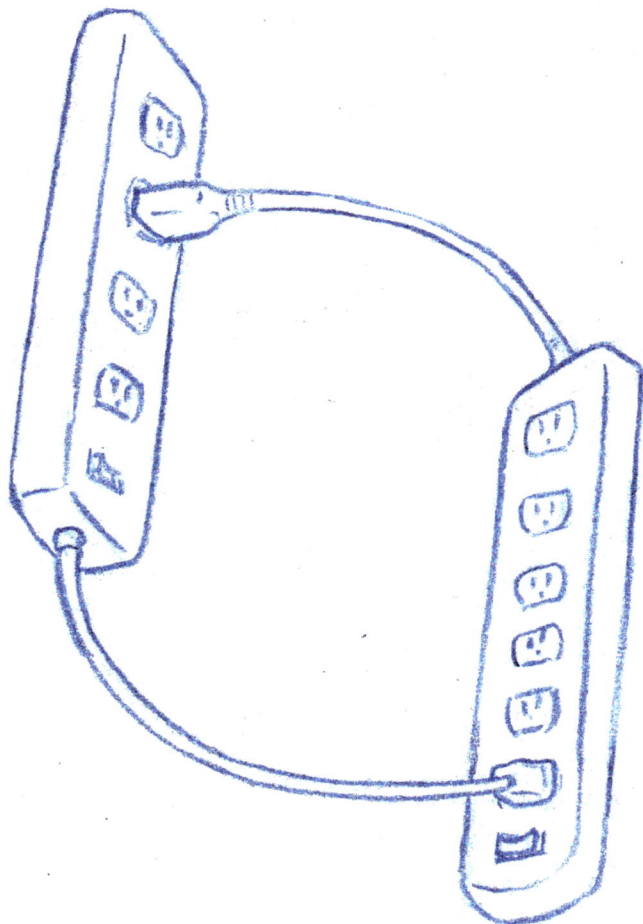

POWER STRUGGLE

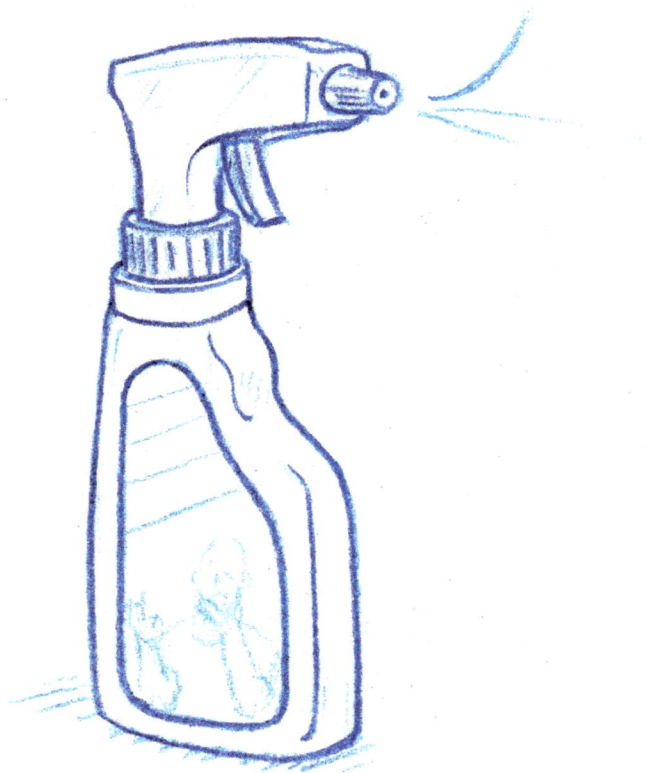

FLOOR-LAMP PROBLEMS

HIGH FIVE

BOING 747

SPOKE OUT

I DON'T UNDERSTAND THE TERM "BUILDINGS".
WE SHOULD PROBABLY BE CALLING THEM "BUILTS."

THE FIRST MEETING OF THE LOCAL PESSIMISTS
CLUB WENT BETTER THAN ANTICIPATED.

SOMETIMES I JUST DON'T FEEL
LIKE FINISHING MY SENT

www.ingramcontent.com/pod-product-compliance
Lightning Source LLC
Chambersburg PA
CBHW041221030426
42336CB00024B/3414